SULLEN EARTH

by

BRENDA FLEET

To those who freed me

She claims
life from the land, singing
to no horizons, skirts long
and wind-blown, grip of
peasant hand on
hip and water-pump.

You settled here
before you can remember;
white memory, impulse,
pull of the land.
You dreamt dark earth,
rich blood; throat of
sand, swallowing dryness.

Visions renew the pulse.
The flesh remains deceived.

Between my fingers, spaces;
a wheel of broken spokes,
a broken wheel. The house
gapes. Grandmother, lost
to me, you singer
of sullen earth.

*

For a lie
they let me be

For my laughter
they gave me pennies

For my look of peace,
token approval

They gave me land
I bartered life

I was a happy victim:
their gifts were several

At first you gave me
only dark contours, twisted
flesh, my birth-cry.
You hovered over me like
a great hawk until
I was forced to look:

the tunnels of your mouth,
flesh upon flesh of lips,
claws in your eyes, hawk-eyed.

You took your prey
gathered by great beaks
from mothers, and mothers before;
glittered your eye all silver:
pressed me to the breast,
proffered your juices, smiling.

Your wings beat against me—
more darkness, shelter,
places of no escape.
                      Then
you gave me a pink dress,
a shuttered house.

*

You ask me to feel at home,
here where there is no home
and no man's stake is driven
firmly into receiving earth.

Here is a soil full of women
who do nothing but weave fragments,
stand by a stove and kettle,
listen for the sound of a man's
axe chopping. Fragments,
unblessed by rain, scattered
pieces of children.

This child at her swing
between porches and clouds,
stories of bears
raiding an icebox:
block of ice, brought from the city,
the bear grumbling, unable.
This child playing at innocence
with private and foreign grief,
the attic to sleep and say rosaries
this black bear the flanks of man,
unknown, desired.

You ask me to stay at home,
beside your water-pump, mother,
your prayers in bed. Deeper
my dreaming, past your needs
towards a greater wanting.

*

He must have been
a hungry man, pushing
his body forwards through
bushes. And when he sat
half-dreaming against trees,
the sound of saws, construction,
cutting and whirring objects,
must have made him grin.
He must have built the house
firmly, with insistence, wanting
to be done.

House as center-stone,
water for the earth,
smiles, angry control.

*

The soil curses its own
growth, curses you and me,
the ancient vision:
                                orchards
filling the eyes, the pale
pink and white of plenty,
streams cool as fish,
stones turning the water.
Ferns, green lace on velvet,
moss wet as woman's thighs,
branches dark and assertive,
thick woods, tree-trunks,
black and singular, light
between many leaves, clearings
fearful with overgrowth, the
smell of pine and birch
lingering. Man's smell,
strong with pleasure, filling
the throat and thighs, heavy,
heaving with union.

The clearing trembles
in its own light; somewhere
a small bird throbs and a wing
lifts and is gone.

The new silence
drives me to arid places.
These visions
forbidden in their joy.

You wrap your shawl closely
about your bosom. Stern
forehead, hands used to
pain, the lean angular
failure.

*

Linger, the smell of man,
you who fashioned me on a crazed
night, a few stars still shining.
Linger, forgotten past, steel
drive, house without man.

I go at night with fistfuls of dirt
to throw at this man my stranger.
I go at night, palms against soil,
and no tears nourish the dry weed.
Feet still and bare as these miles,
land of no dark and green trees.

*

His leaving
a fact
brutal
as earth
as sky
meeting earth
and no man
in the distance
waving,

this horizon
this long stretch:
earth,
forever,
not joining
the sky

*

Mother wails and her many sisters
discover lovers in chevrolets
and grandmother's fist drops
to her side, she stares at nothing.

The women laugh with several men.

A gash in the land, a dry wound:
the taste acrid between lips,
mouth ravaged. Hips ache with
fatherless children; nights cold;
barren, you bear only me.

I do not redeem the soil.
I sell my birthright.

The women slowly die, and so the soil
We laugh, we show our breasts
We die in parked cars

*

This house in August,
in late August, is
unfit for life. Snow
comes over the river,
without prophecy. The
sudden cold is not
kept out by windows.
Noise turns inside
this house. Plans
to leave, to go elsewhere,
are made. Nobody
goes elsewhere. The August
wind leans inward with weight.
No walls have fallen. Plans
continue, imperatives
to go outside, to go
anywhere else. For a walk.
To the beach of stones.
To see a boat, a bird
in flight before winter.

Night
is never soon enough,
taking away whiteness,
too many highways
of white doom. The
blackness is never
thorough enough.

I file my nails down. And
they grow. This house grows,
distant from cities.

My life is out of my hands.
Others, below, devise routes
for my hands to follow.
Their voices
scatter me into
unknown voyages;
eyes like compasses
whirl and plot
the skeletal direction
of my fingers.

Never remain in a house
which is dangerous to the soul.

I hear and ignore
my own plea, its
urgency. There is
much talk. We
cannot decide to go,
so many calendars
prevent us. I have said
good-bye so often, with
packed suitcases, and
dreamed you would take me:

into my own horror,
sleeping,
I have taken you.

My breathing becomes
someone ele's moans,
less recognizable.
I am salt water, fetus,
avoiding light.
One hundred white leaves
hit the window;
this house
grasps and keeps us,
every one.

Occasional footsteps
on dirt road. Bats
follow the light, crazed
and utterly blinded.

O my fragmentation,
fragmented family,
fearing truth and anger.
And each undone.
In white fall
weather, only
my nightmare screams.

*

I take leave of the old house,
cold rooms and receding spiders,
the falling beams. It is time.

I searched for you in scattered
birds on a porch, the March
brightness of feathers, snow,
my window open to sky and trees.

Your shadow
crossed the rooms and left.

Later, in cities, I looked at
white walls and wondered.
Perhaps I recovered you by
calling your name, you answered.

Then this old house. Barren
with you tearing my body from
mind, dissociation. I'm dividing
your things from mine, seeing us
splitting apart.
    Dreams, melancholy,
unreason of gray afternoons, all
must be packaged, marked, in order.

I'm tidying a small lifetime,
crossing a river: another self
waiting to claim the boxes, opening
the screaming air and letting loose
all manner of nightmare, blackness,
another Pandora seeking rebirth.

*

love, your warm body
silent and threatened beside me
I hold the force of knives

love, I weep for your arms
as child, earth, flower
and the sun gone.

*